A Family of Donkeys

Heiderose and Andreas Fischer-Nagel

A & C Black · London

Contents

To our children, Tamarica and Cosmea Désiree

A & C Black (Publishers) Limited
35 Bedford Row
London WC1R 4JH
This edition © 1988 A & C Black (Publishers) Limited.

Originally published in German under the title
'Das Eselbuch' © 1988 by Kinderbuchverlag KBV
Luzern AG

Acknowledgements
The publishers would like to thank Michael Chinery
for his help and advice.
The pictures on pages 12–15 are by Dorothy Morris

A CIP catalogue record for this book is available
from the British Library.

ISBN 0-7136-3125-2

Typeset by Method Ltd, Epping, Essex
Printed in West Germany

Introducing donkeys

Donkeys are intelligent and sweet-natured – not the stupid, obstinate fools that some people think. They make good pets and safe playmates. A donkey will let you hug it, pat it and tickle behind its ears.

Donkeys were first domesticated about 6,000 years ago in Africa, and later brought to Europe. People kept them for riding and to carry heavy loads. But in return for all their hard work, donkeys were often kicked, beaten and half-starved.

Donkeys not only work hard, but they've also been significant in history. On Palm Sunday, Jesus rode a donkey into Jerusalem. People say that's why donkeys have the marks of a cross on their backs.

We live in Germany and we have three donkeys. Our donkey-keeping began when we were on holiday in the north of the country. One day, we came across a little herd of donkeys grazing in a meadow. The donkeys were inquisitive, and one of them gently nibbled us, to say hello. The time had come, we decided, to have a donkey of our own as a pet.

Griselda

We chose our donkey from the herd. It wasn't easy to decide between all the different colours: fawn, brown, piebald and grey. But at last we spotted the one we wanted – a pretty little female donkey, or jenny, with a soft grey coat, and the cross on her back marked in dark, ruler-straight lines. We named our donkey Griselda.

7

Neddy

Until Griselda came, the big meadow behind our house had only been occupied by a cock and four hens. Griselda shared the meadow with them, but they weren't very good company.

Sometimes Griselda would let out a long, loud bray. Was she lonely? When a neighbouring farmer offered us a male donkey, or jack, we accepted straight away. The jack's name was Neddy. That's him, in the picture on the right.

eddy was about the same size as riselda, but his head was broader. His at felt like silk, and his eyes were large nd gentle-looking. We loved Neddy from e moment we first saw him, but how ould Griselda react?

When they met, Neddy was very interested in Griselda, and sniffed her again and again. But Griselda ignored her new companion. Although Neddy tried to attract her attention, she went on ignoring him … until, one day, she came into season.

When a female animal comes into season, it means she's ready to mate with the male. Female donkeys come into season every three weeks during the spring and occasionally at other times of the year.

ating and pregnancy

riselda was excited. She
ewed, snapped at the air
d spat. She kept backing
wards Neddy. At first,
eddy screamed and
shed away. But when
riselda stood still at last,
e got up on his back legs
d mounted her. Then
eddy and Griselda mated.
twelve months' time, a
al would be born.

uring the first half of the
egnancy, we could see no
ange in Griselda. She
as now friendly towards
eddy, and they grazed in
e meadow side by side.

hen, gradually, we noticed
riselda's appetite
owing. After about nine
onths, she became
unded-looking. She
oved awkwardly and
sted more than usual. She
eferred to stay in or near
e shed, and walked
refully, to make sure she
dn't slip.

Birth

It's now a year since the mating. Griselda's udder is swollen and tight. One day we notice that both teats are dripping. That means the birth will soon take place.

We go out and look at Griselda at regular intervals. Although it's a warm night, she's chosen to give birth in the shed. She's standing still in the corner. When we lay our hands on her sides, we can feel movement. This could mean indigestion, or colic, or it could be just the unborn foal moving about. Griselda looks round at her sides.

Then Griselda seems to feel sudden pains. She flops down in the straw. Her labour has begun.

During labour, the muscles contract and relax to push the foal out of its mother's body. Just before four o'clock in the morning, we see a sort of bubble beginning to be pushed out. It looks like a plastic bag full of water. It's the bag that the foal's been developing in, inside Griselda's womb.

Now the foal's head and front legs appear, and the bag tears open. After more pushing, the foal's whole body – still partly wrapped in the bag – slips out on to the straw.

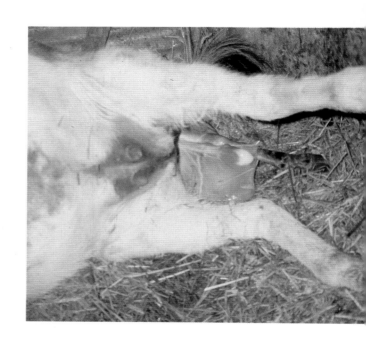

The umbilical cord breaks

The birth has lasted just half an hour.
Neddy realizes what has happened, and
brays with excitement.

The foal is lying, wet and exhausted, in
the straw. Griselda is exhausted too, but
she manages to stand up. This breaks the
umbilical cord, which joined the foal to its
mother while it was in the womb. Some
animals, such as cats, have to bite
through the cord to break it.

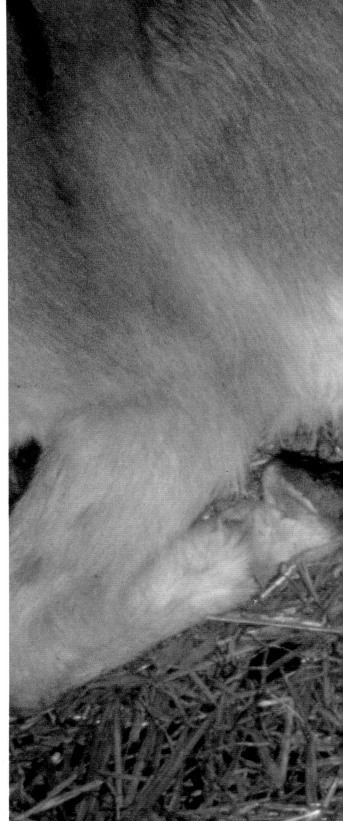

The foal stands up

The new-born foal still looks rather crumpled. It blinks at the electric light in the shed. Everything seems bright and cold to it, after the soft, warm darkness of its mother's womb. Now it has to breathe by itself for the first time.

 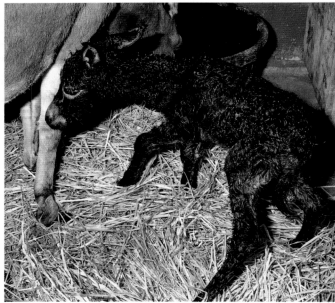

The foal's first smell is its mother. It will always be able to recognize her by her smell. We let it sniff our hands, so that it will think of us as friends, too. Meanwhile, Griselda is licking it clean and dry. The foal is female – a filly – and we're going to call her Twinkle.

Only a quarter of an hour after being born, Twinkle is already trying to get up. Her legs are like wobbly stilts, but she's soon standing, all the same. She nudges her mother, looking for the udder. There – she's found it! Twinkle eagerly sucks the milk.

17

Twinkle leaves the shed

All hoofed animals, such as donkeys, struggle to their feet almost as soon as they're born. They have to be strong to survive.

In the wild, new-born donkeys have to be able to move on straight away, with the herd. If they're too weak to get up, they won't be able to escape from dangers that may threaten them.

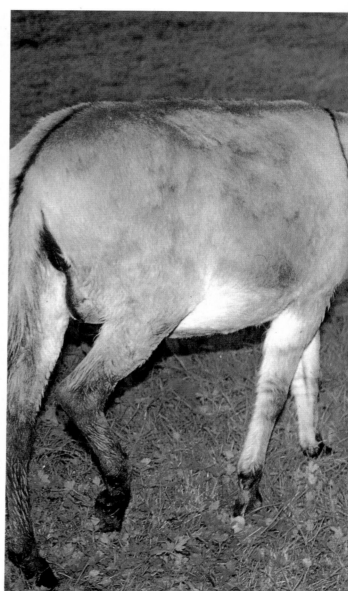

e mother donkey's milk makes the foal
ow strong. The milk is especially good
 the foal in the first four days, because
en it contains special substances which
lp to stop the foal falling ill.

When Twinkle is only a few hours old, she
follows Griselda out into the meadow.
Neddy is waiting for them. He carefully
sniffs Twinkle. From now on, he will be
watching over his little family.

We leave Griselda to clean Twinkle. In the morning, when we come out again, Twinkle is all dry and fuzzy. The woolly fur on her head looks like a hat over her eyes.

Our daughter meets Twinkle now for the first time, and picks her up. Twinkle weighs fourteen kilograms – about four times as much as a human baby. Griselda trusts us not to harm her foal, but she's still very watchful.

Twinkle is eight hours old

Twinkle is 65 centimetres high, from the ground to the top of her shoulders, where the black line of her cross comes down. She's just eight hours old, but already prancing around the meadow. Within three days, she'll be eating grass, as well as drinking her mother's milk.

Although donkey foals eat grass so early on, for a long time they have only their small, milk teeth. Their adult teeth don't grow for four or five years. These second teeth are constantly worn down, and keep on growing back for the rest of the donkey's life.

Twinkle tires easily

Griselda pushes Twinkle about quite roughly, with her nose, to keep her on the move. Movement is important for Twinkle, because it helps her digestive system to work properly.

Sometimes Twinkle dodges her mother's nudging nose, and scampers away to play by herself. But as she's so young, she quickly tires. She lies down on the grass and falls asleep. It looks as if she must be dreaming that she's still running about, because her legs kick and twitch every now and then.

Donkeys have moods

A donkey must have company. If it doesn't live with other donkeys, then human company will do. But if it's left completely alone, a donkey will be very unhappy.

Donkeys have always worked hard – and with good will – for people. They are stubborn only if they are overworked or frightened. Horses bolt when frightened, but donkeys just dig their heels into the ground and refuse to budge!

You can tell a donkey's mood by its ears. If they are lying flat back – even flatter than Twinkle's, in the picture below – then it's probably in a bad mood. Don't try to pat it, or it might nip you. When a donkey dozes, it will hang its head, often with one ear up and one ear down.

Twinkle plays

Twinkle frolics in the meadow. She dashes wildl here and there and round i circles, but she never stray far from her mother. Sometimes she teases Griselda by nipping her flanks or even trying to jump on her back.

Twinkle flings her back legs into the air, or speeds along flat out, with her head down. She can turn sharply or stop dead, even in mid-gallop.

So much rushing about in the fresh air makes Twink hungry. Occasionally, she stops to suck Griselda's milk or to nibble some blades of grass.

Twinkle meets the dog

Twinkle doesn't find it much fun playing with Griselda, because Griselda won't chase about with her. But it's different when she meets our dog, Lisa.

First of all, Twinkle is curious, and a bit nervous. The two strangers sniff each other uncertainly. Then Twinkle blows suddenly into Lisa's face. Lisa becomes excited, and licks Twinkle's nose. Now dog and donkey are friends.

Twinkle and Lisa race across the meadow together. Twinkle can go much faster because of her long legs, but Lisa doesn't seem to mind.

Having a dust bath

Griselda keeps Twinkle clean by licking her all over every day. Twinkle must just stand still and be patient.

Donkeys very rarely bathe in water, but they love dust baths. In the bottom picture, you can see Griselda showing Twinkle how it's done.

Griselda is lying down on a bare patch of ground in the meadow. She rolls over on her back and wriggles. At last she gets up again, covered in dry, powdery earth, and puffing heavily. The dust soaks up sweat and grease and cleans her coat.

Then Griselda nudges Twinkle until she too lies down in the dust. She rolls around just like her mother. It hasn't taken her long to learn.

Twinkle is a year old

Twinkle grows quickly. It's now a year since her birth, and she's almost as big as her mother. But her coat is still much softer than Griselda's.

Mother and foal seem less close than at first. Twinkle often wanders off on her own in the meadow, and Griselda is less watchful than before. She even pushes Twinkle away when Twinkle tries to nuzzle up to her. Griselda knows that Twinkle is old enough now to look after herself.

Griselda has mated again and is expecting another foal. We could now sell Twinkle, if we wanted to: she stopped needing her mother's milk when she was six months old. But we've decided to keep her. Twinkle has become one of the family, and we couldn't bear to let her go.

Donkeys in other countries

For many centuries, donkeys have been harnessed to carts or made to carry heavy loads on their backs. Today, donkeys in Britain are usually kept as pets, but in other countries they are still kept as useful workers. The top left picture here shows a donkey in Spain. Spanish donkeys are very big and strong.

The top right picture was taken in one of the Arab countries, where donkeys are often more common than cars or buses.

The picture on the left will give you an idea of the kind of wild donkeys that domestic donkeys are descended from. The breed in the picture comes from Africa, but these two live in a zoo.

Mules and hinnies

Donkeys and horses are very similar in lots of ways. Their close similarity means that they can cross-breed. If a male donkey mates with a female horse or pony, then the foal will be a mule. You can see some mules in the left-hand picture, below. (Only the animal out in front isn't a mule: it's a pony.)

If a female donkey mates with a male horse or pony, their foal will be a hinny. It's a hinny coming down the path towards you in the right-hand picture. For simplicity, you can lump together mules and hinnies, and call them all mules.

Mules and hinnies are always infertile. That means they can't have foals themselves.

Donkeys and horses

Horses, ponies, donkeys – and even zebras – are all members of the horse family. They all have hooves. A horse's or donkey's hoof is a kind of large, tough fingernail.

In the wild, horses and donkeys usually live in herds. The herd is always on the alert for danger, and each animal has an excellent sense of hearing and smell.

Horses and donkeys are similar in lots of ways, but there are important differences between them. For instance, a herd of horses is always led by a stallion – a male horse – but a herd of donkeys is led by a female. Donkey foals grow up much more quickly than horse foals.

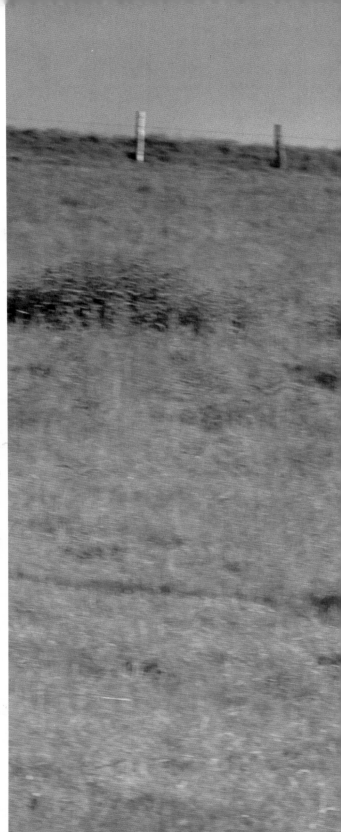

A pet donkey needs lots of kindness and attention. In return, it will trust you, and be a patient, faithful friend. Griselda, Neddy and Twinkle have taught us that people are wrong to call donkeys stupid and stubborn. Donkeys are rewarding to look after and exciting to bring up from birth. We can't wait for Griselda to have her next foal.

Index